WHAT CAN YOU DO?

A BOOK ABOUT DISCOVERING WHAT YOU DO WELL

BY SHELLEY ROTNER AND SHEILA KELLY, Ed.D.

PHOTOGRAPHS BY SHELLEY ROTNER

THE MILLBROOK PRESS M BROOKFIELD, CONNECTICUT

"I know a boy
WHO CAN DRAW
very well

and a girl who can

CLIMB VERY HIGH."

"I like to SWIM
and learned how to FLOAT,

but my little brother
is better on skis."

We're happy when we
DO SOMETHING WELL,
whatever that might be.

"REAdING IS EASY
for me,
but I'd like to be better at math."

"I CAN'T READ
very well yet. I wish I could."

It can take a long time
to be good at something.

Marie knows how to spell,
Jill prints well,
and Gene is really good
with computers.

"I HAVEN'T
DISCOVERED
what I'm good at yet."

Nathan writes stories.
Beth likes to build.

"I made the soccer team."

"I see lots of things in the park."

We all like to do

WHAT WE DO BEST.

And when things are hard, we need
HELP TO LEARN.

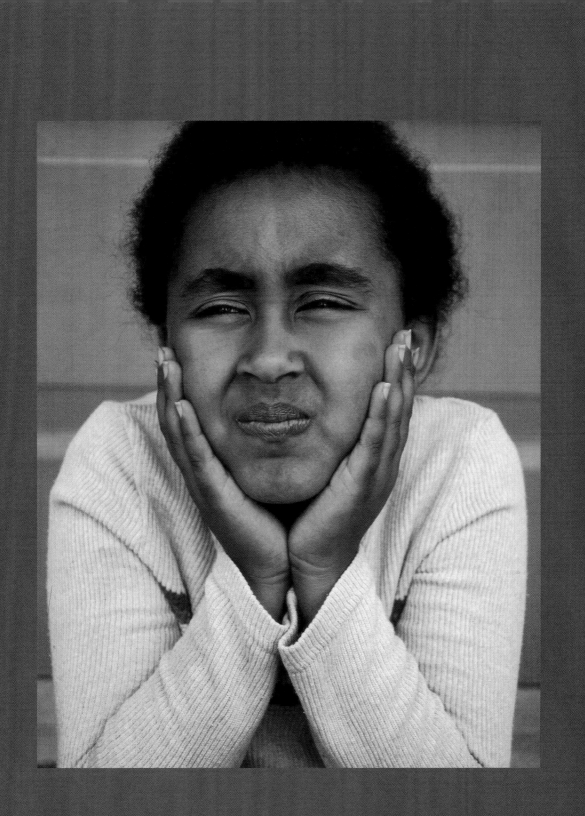

"I DON'T GET IT."

WE'RE GOOD
at different things.

"I feed the baby myself now."

"I can fix my brother's wagon."

"I got my training wheels off early."

"The kids made me

CAPTAIN
OF OUR TEAM."

Schoolwork, acting, singing, dancing, playing games or sports!

We all have something

WE DO WELL.

WHAT CAN YOU DO?

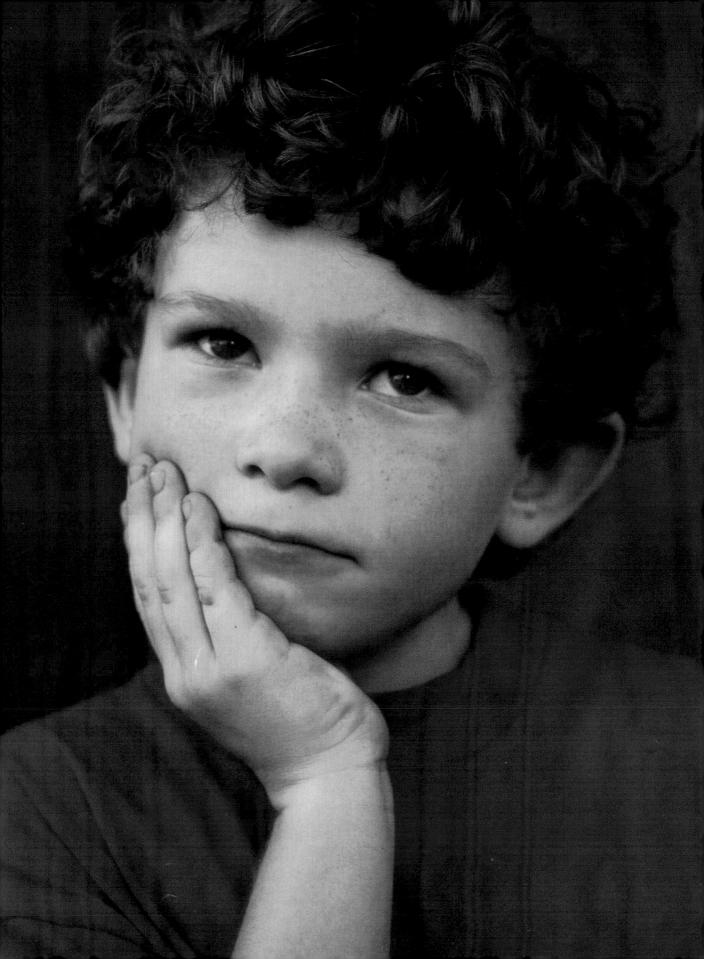

A NOTE FOR PARENTS AND TEACHERS

Psychologist Dr. Howard Gardner, in an extensive project at Harvard, has led in the study of how we assess and appreciate different kinds of intelligence. His teaching has inspired new ways of assessing children's abilities and enriched the content of progressive school curricula. Our appreciation of Dr. Gardner's work informed the creation of this book.

In his book, *Frames of Mind*, Dr. Gardner argues that there are at least seven relatively independent kinds of intelligence, which he documents through careful psychological and cross-cultural study. The first of these is **linguistic intelligence**, the sensitivity to word choice and usage, demonstrated by poets and valued in all branches of study within the humanities. It is the intelligence valued early in the traditional classroom. **Logical-mathematical intelligence**, the ability to abstract and generalize the relationship of numbers in order to arrive at a more abstract level of thought and understanding, is also highly valued in the academic world.

Many people relate exceptional ability in music to logical-mathematical intelligence but Gardner sees musical ability as a unique form of intelligence. He identifies **musical intelligence** as a capacity to grasp the patterns of sound (tones) and rhythms and reproduce them or create new ones. Dr. Gardner designates a fourth form of intelligence, **spatial intelligence**, understood as a visual-spatial capacity.

According to Gardner's theory, the ability to use one's body in highly differentiated and skilled ways and the capacity to work expressively with objects describe **bodily-kinesthetic intelligence**. What may be thought of as social intelligence or an ability to understand human feelings and interactions, Gardner describes as two forms of **personal intelligences**, the capacity to assess one's own feelings, and the capacity to notice and make distinctions among other individuals.

In this book, we hope to provide children and the adults who care for them a chance to think and talk about the ways children have met with success or difficulty in using their abilities. We hope to help them recognize that one ability is not better than another, and we wish them delight in their strengths and freedom to seek help with their challenges.

— SHEILA M. KELLY, ED.D.

Library of Congress Cataloging-in-Publication Data

Rotner, Shelley.
What can you do? : a book about discovering what you do well / by Shelley Rotner and Sheila Kelly ; photographs by Shelley Rotner.
p. cm.
ISBN 0-7613-2119-5 (lib. bdg.)
1. Ability in children—Juvenile literature. [1. Ability. 2. Individuality.] I. Kelly, Sheila M. II. Title.

BF723.A25 .R68 2000
153.9—dc21
00-041878

Especially for Nell and kids like her who are discovering what they do well. —S.M.K.

For Emily, who can do so many things well. — S.R.

Published by The Millbrook Press, Inc.
2 Old New Milford Road   Brookfield, CT 06804
www.millbrookpress.com
Copyright © 2001 by Shelley Rotner and Sheila Kelly
Photographs copyright © 2001 by Shelley Rotner
All rights reserved.
Printed in the United States of America
Designed by Carolyn Eckert
5 4 3 2 1